maybe we should avocuddle

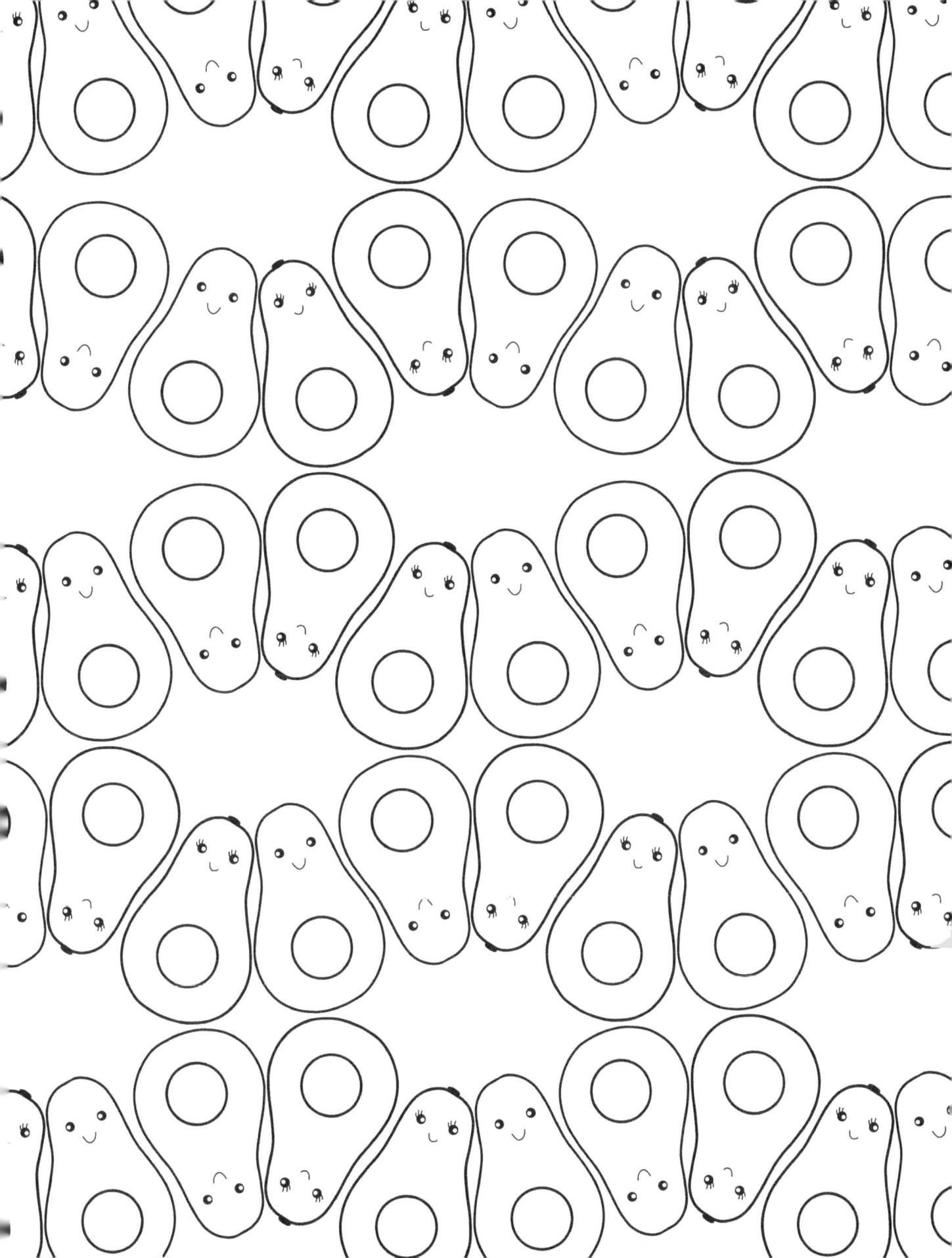

Envelope Instructions
Cut along bold line.
Fold along dotted lines. Fold side flaps in.
Use glue or tape to secure bottom flap to side flaps.
Insert card. Fold top flap down and seal with glue or tape.

BOTTOM FLAP

you are so berry sweet!

Envelope Instructions
Cut along bold line.
Fold along dotted lines. Fold side flaps in.
Use glue or tape to secure bottom flap to side flaps.
Insert card. Fold top flap down and seal with glue or tape.

BOTTOM FLAP

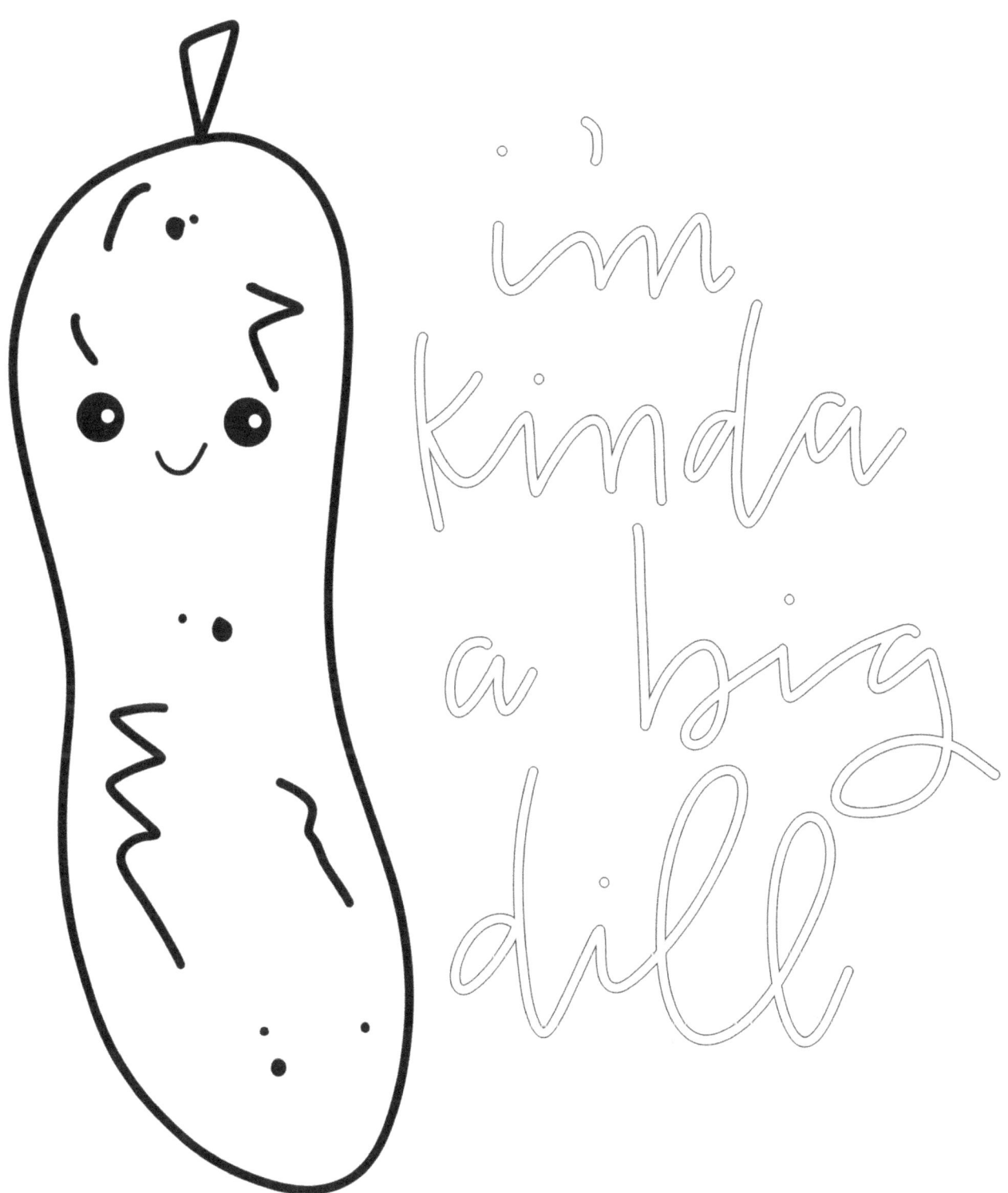

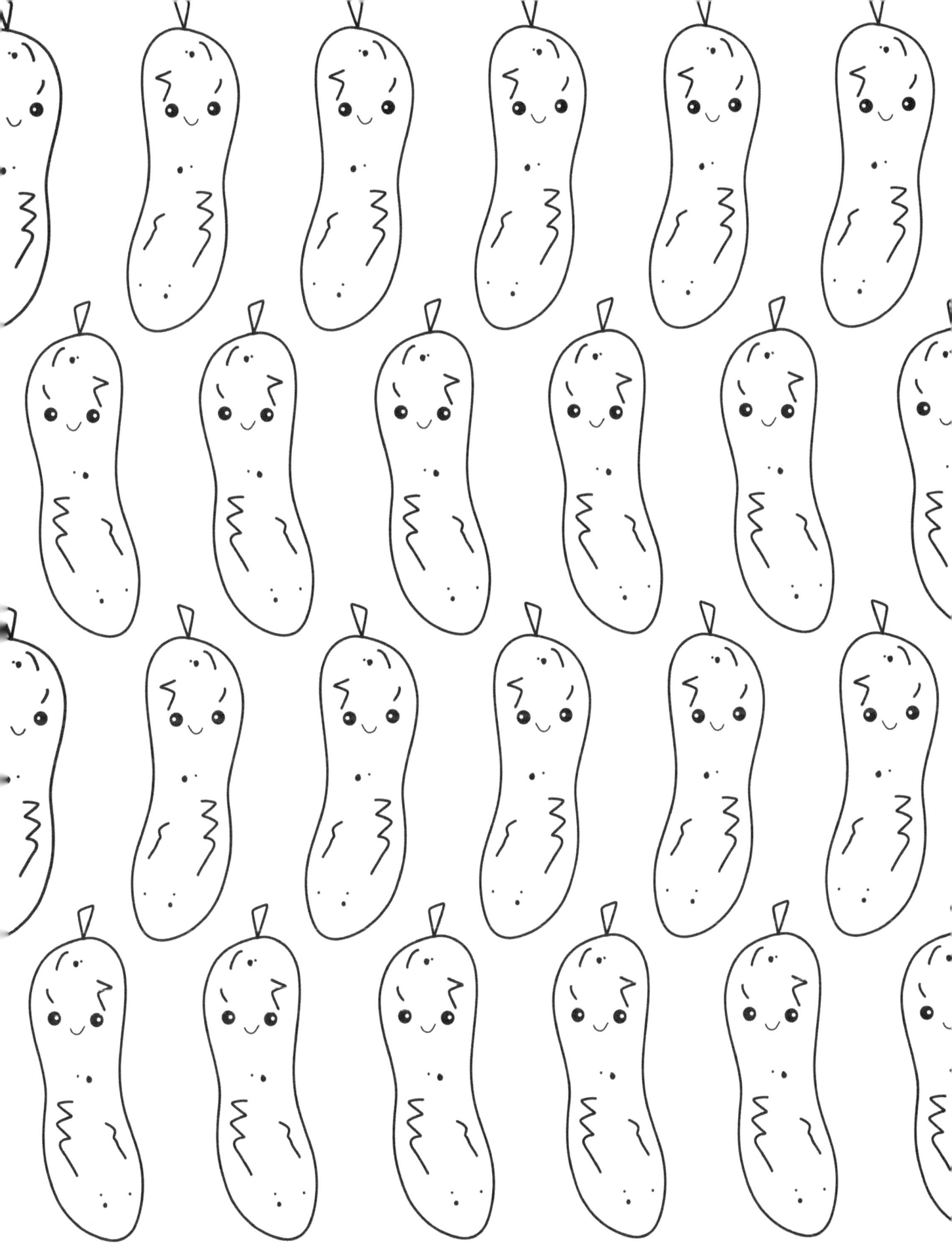

Envelope Instructions

Cut along bold line.
Fold along dotted lines. Fold side flaps in.
Use glue or tape to secure bottom flap to side flaps.
Insert card. Fold top flap down and seal with glue or tape.

BOTTOM FLAP

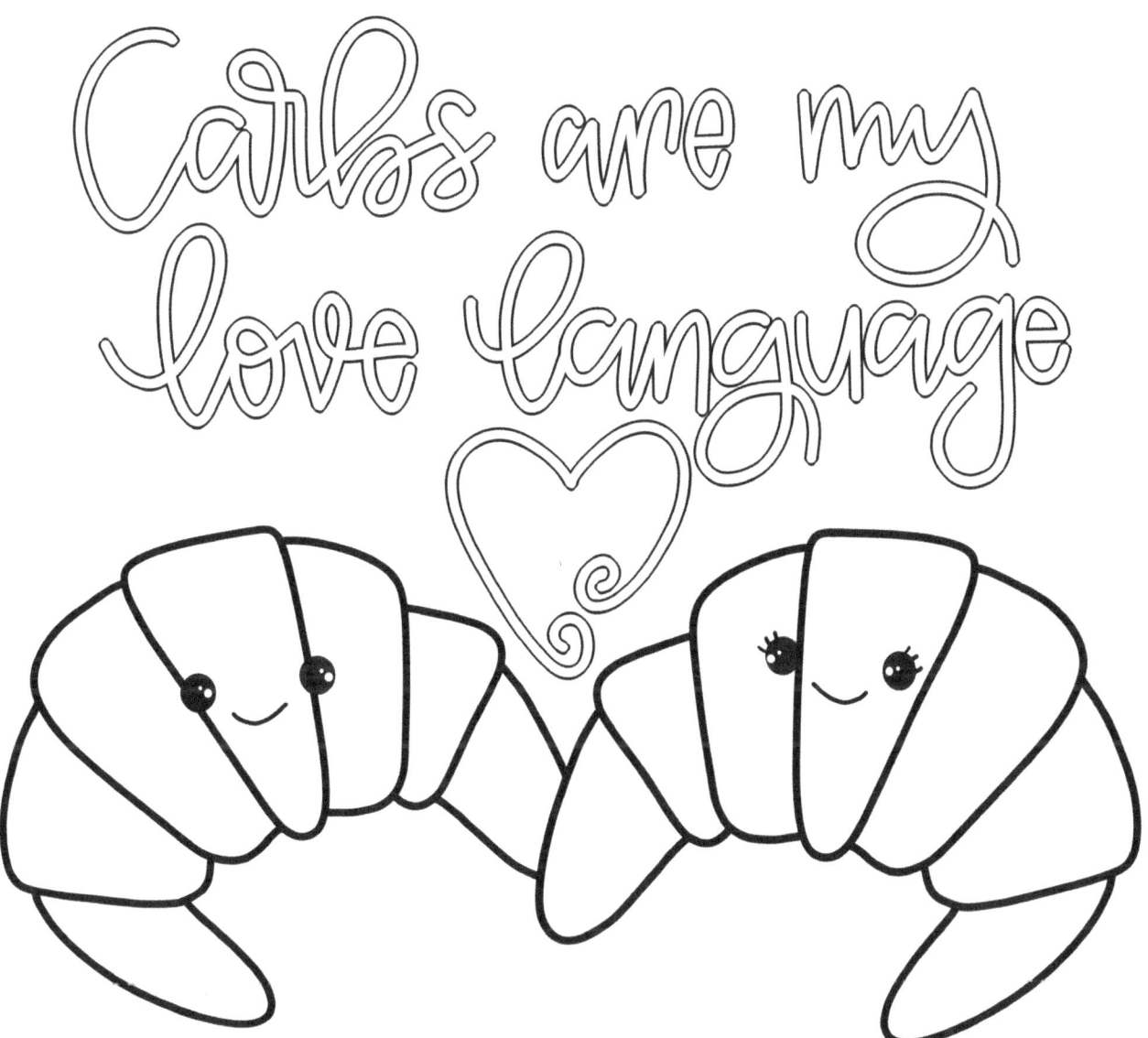

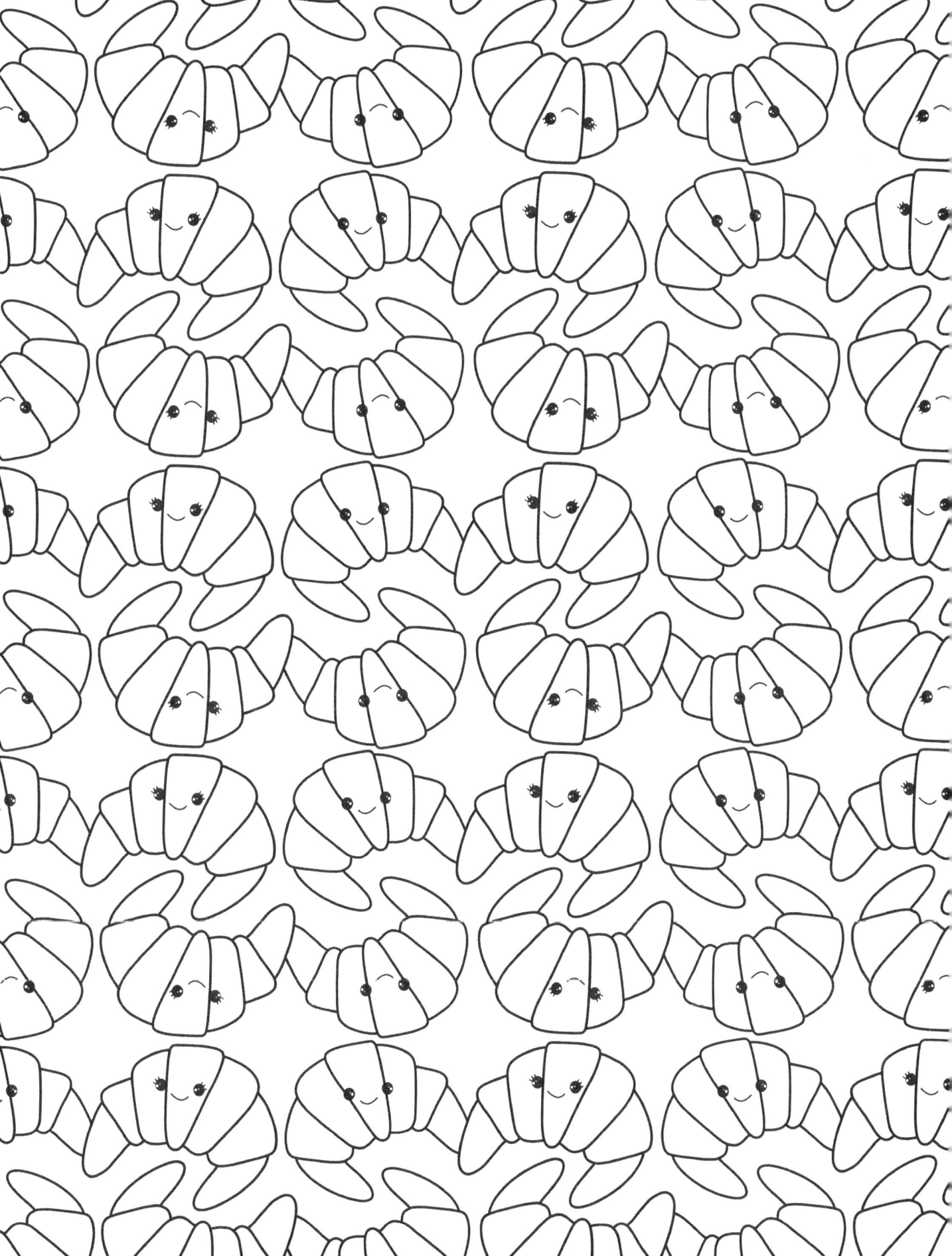

Envelope Instructions
Cut along bold line.
Fold along dotted lines. Fold side flaps in.
Use glue or tape to secure bottom flap to side flaps.
Insert card. Fold top flap down and seal with glue or tape.

BOTTOM FLAP

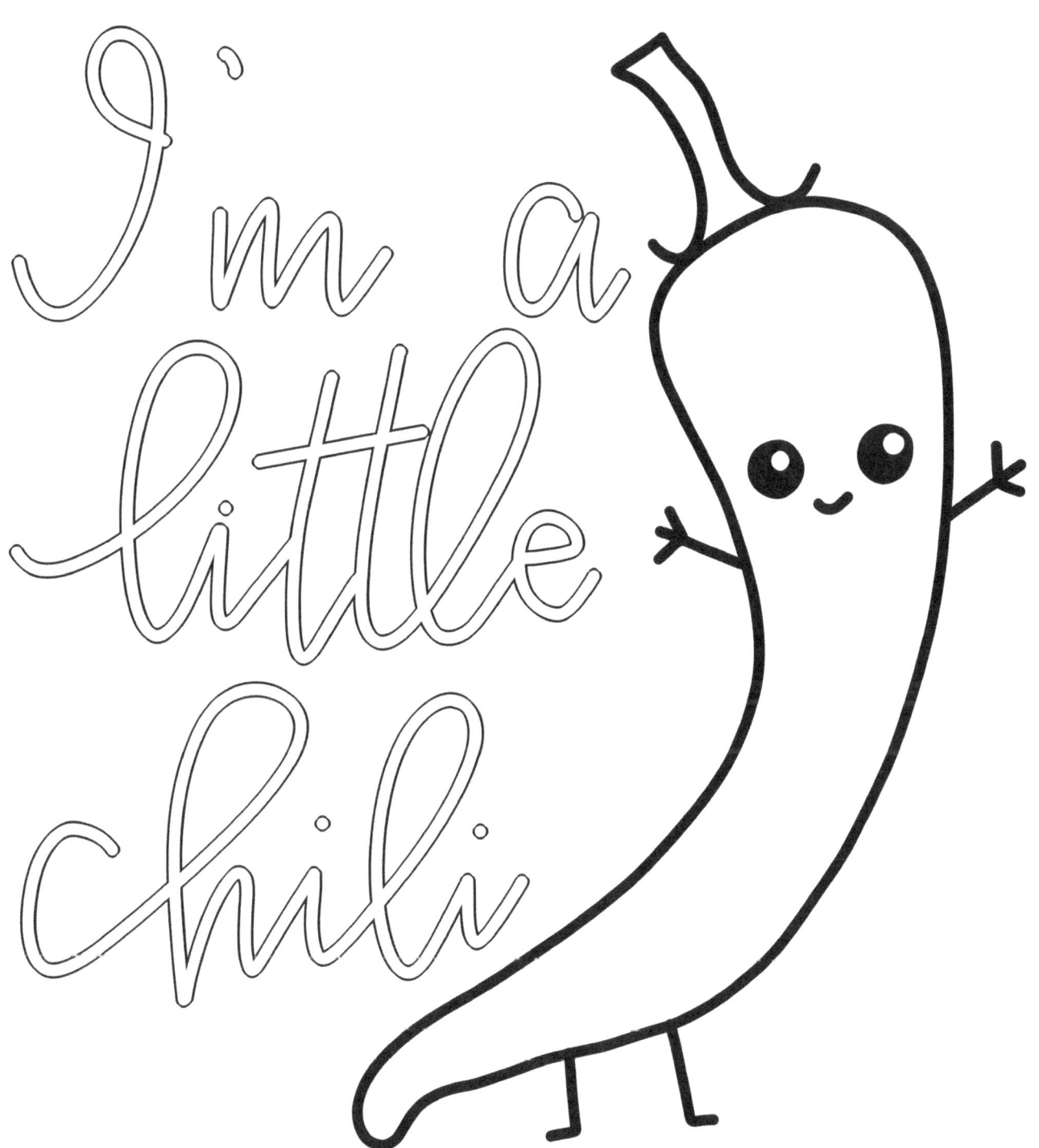

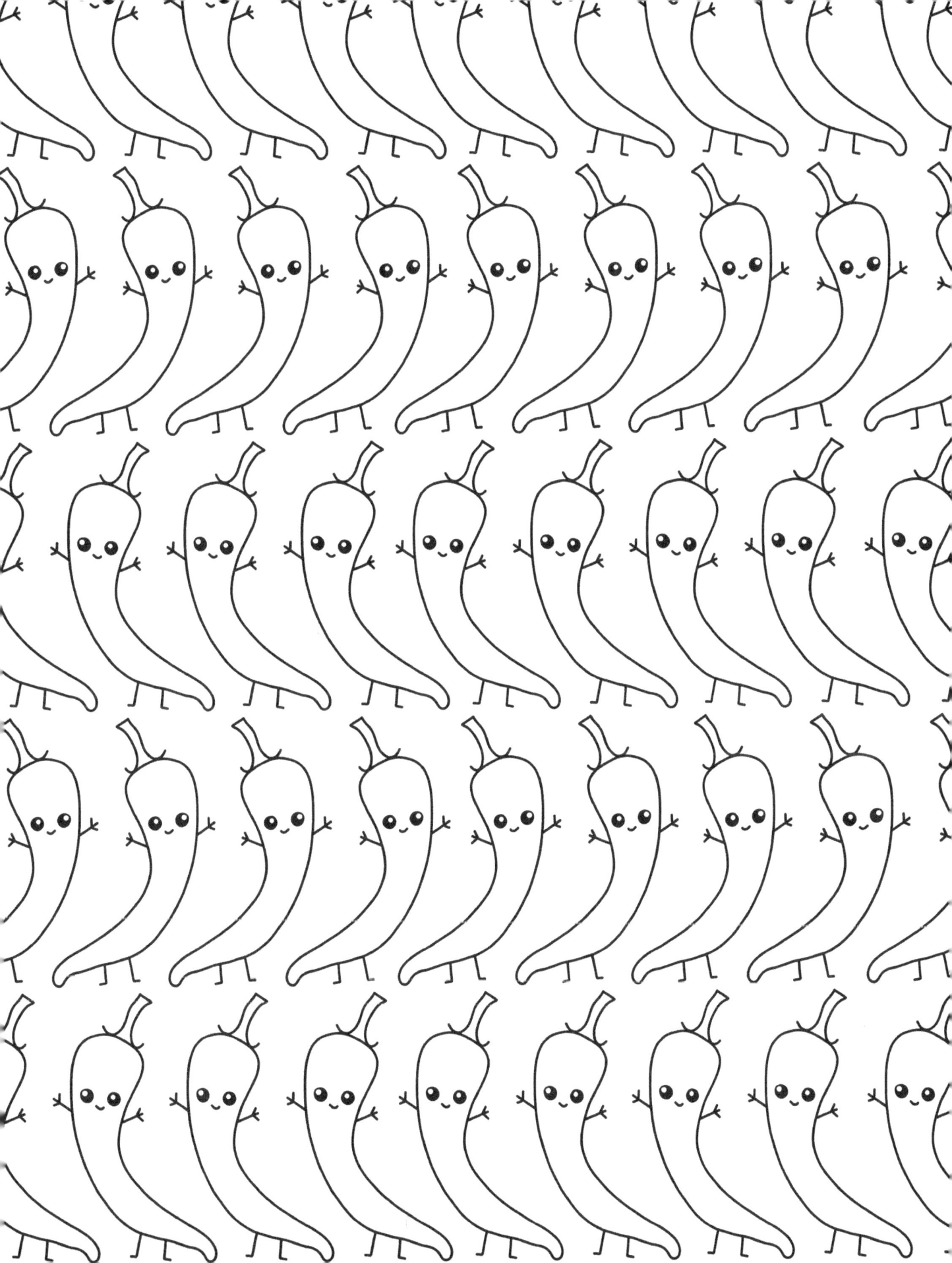

Envelope Instructions

Cut along bold line.
Fold along dotted lines. Fold side flaps in.
Use glue or tape to secure bottom flap to side flaps.
Insert card. Fold top flap down and seal with glue or tape.

BOTTOM FLAP

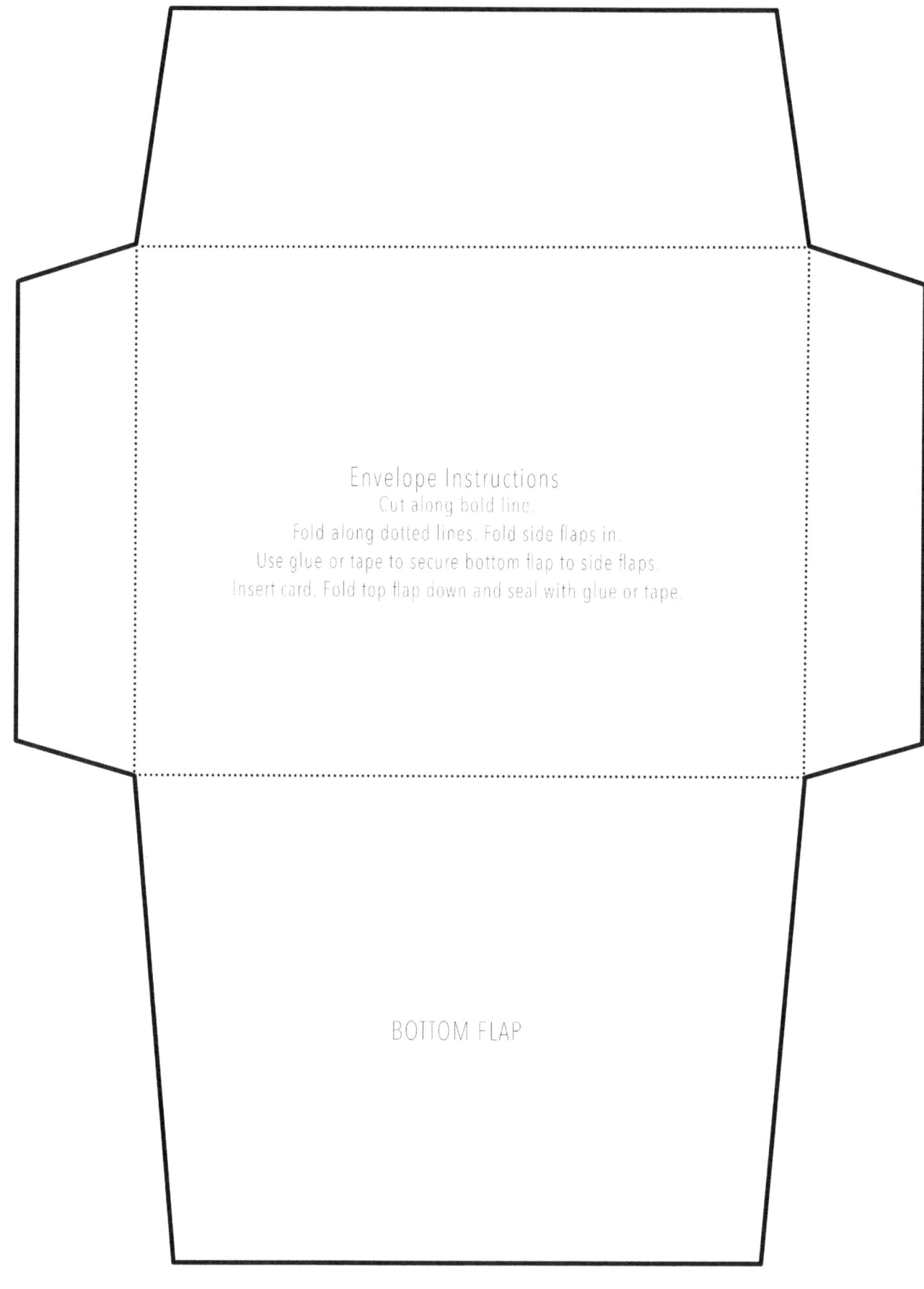

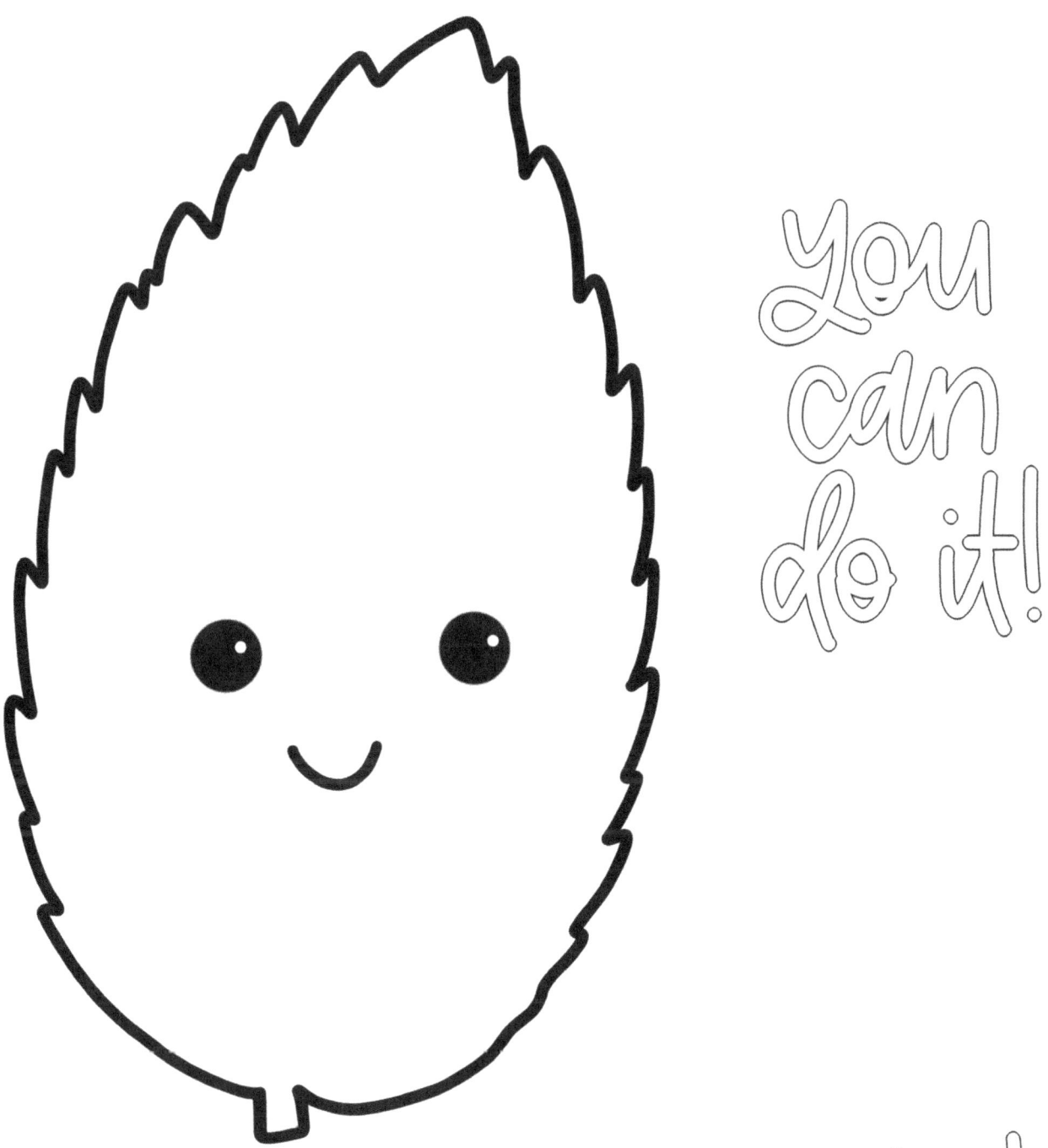

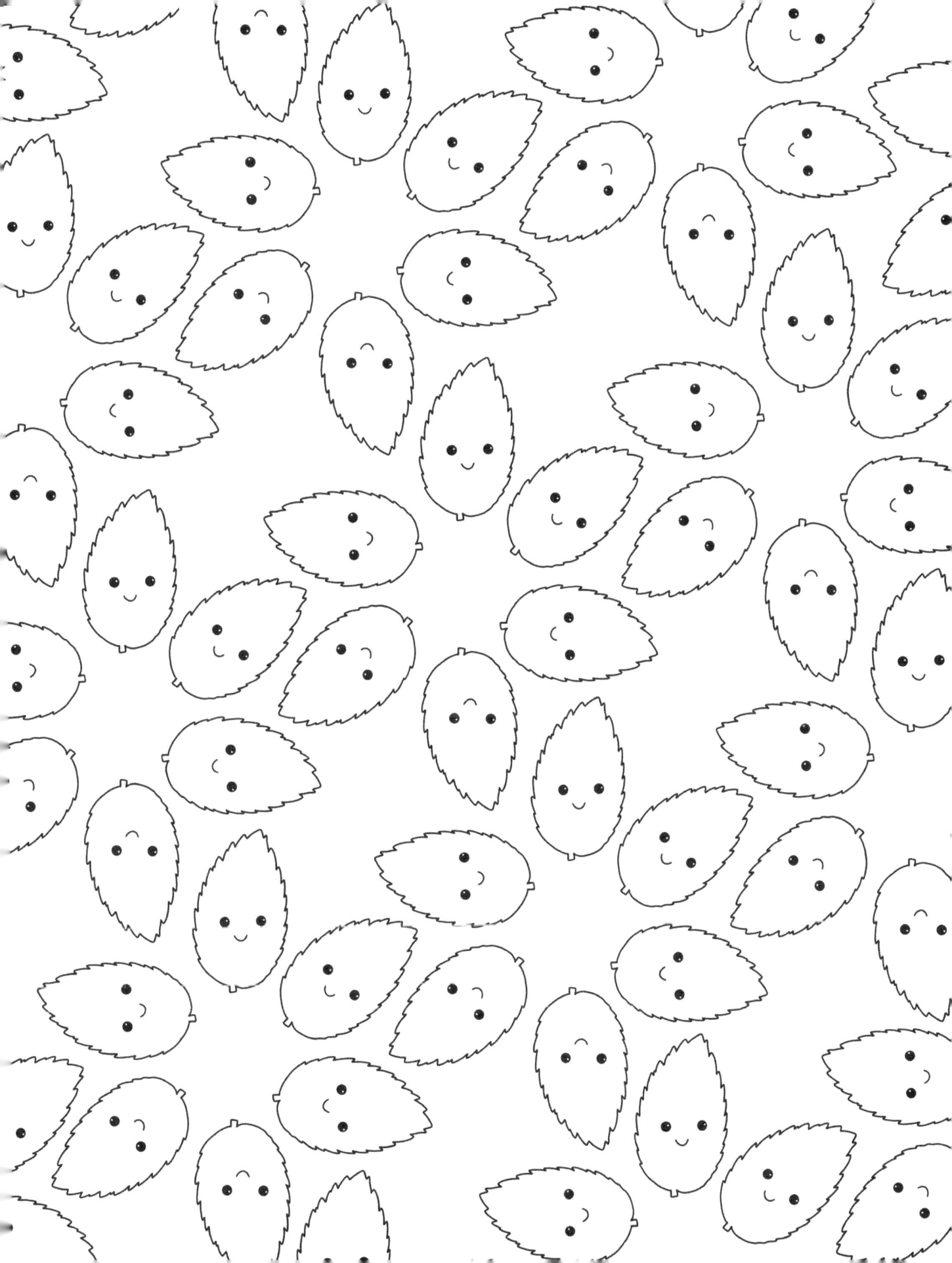

Envelope Instructions
Cut along bold line.
Fold along dotted lines. Fold side flaps in.
Use glue or tape to secure bottom flap to side flaps.
Insert card. Fold top flap down and seal with glue or tape.

BOTTOM FLAP

have a gouda day!

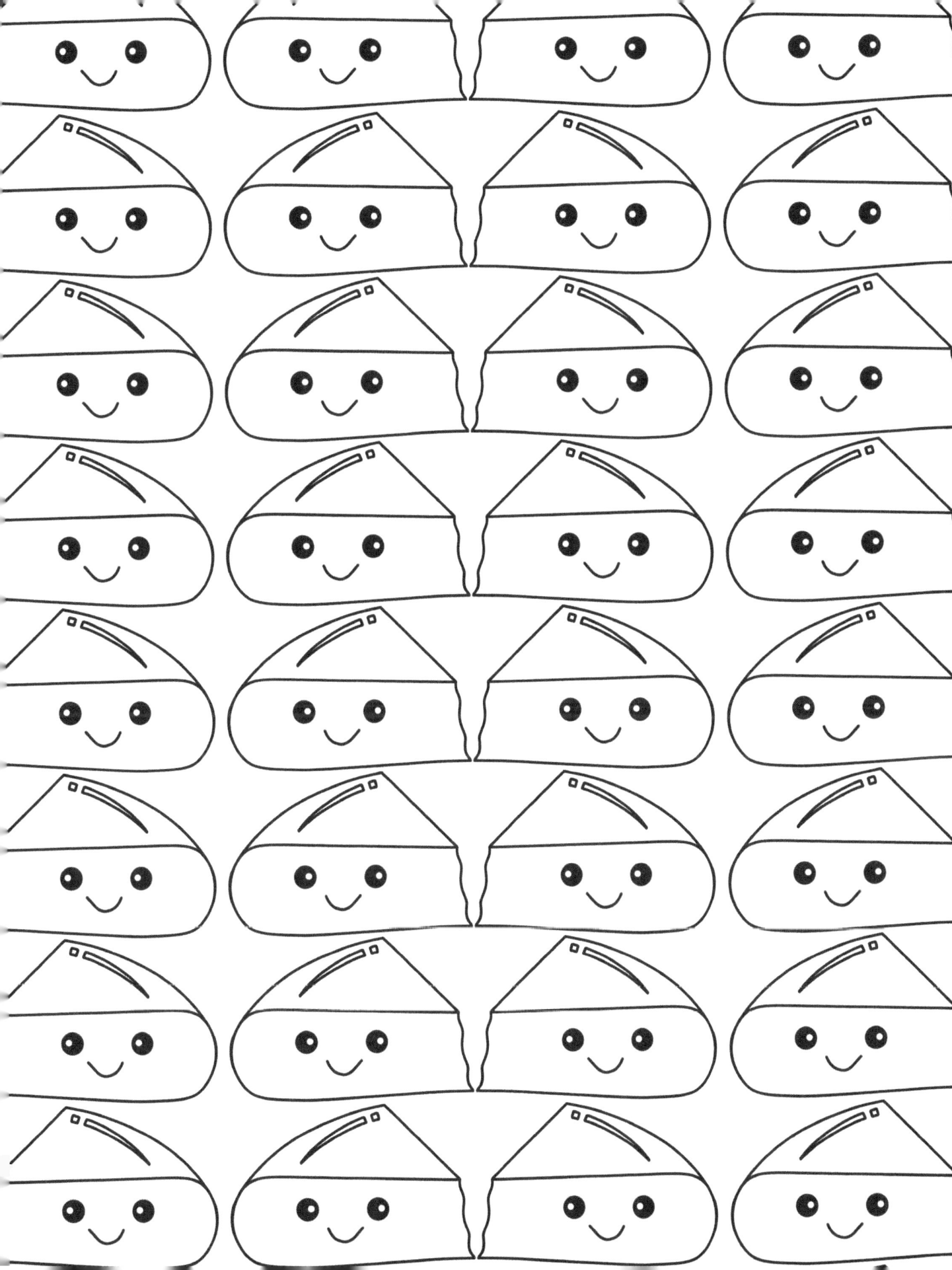

Envelope Instructions

Cut along bold line.
Fold along dotted lines. Fold side flaps in.
Use glue or tape to secure bottom flap to side flaps.
Insert card. Fold top flap down and seal with glue or tape.

BOTTOM FLAP

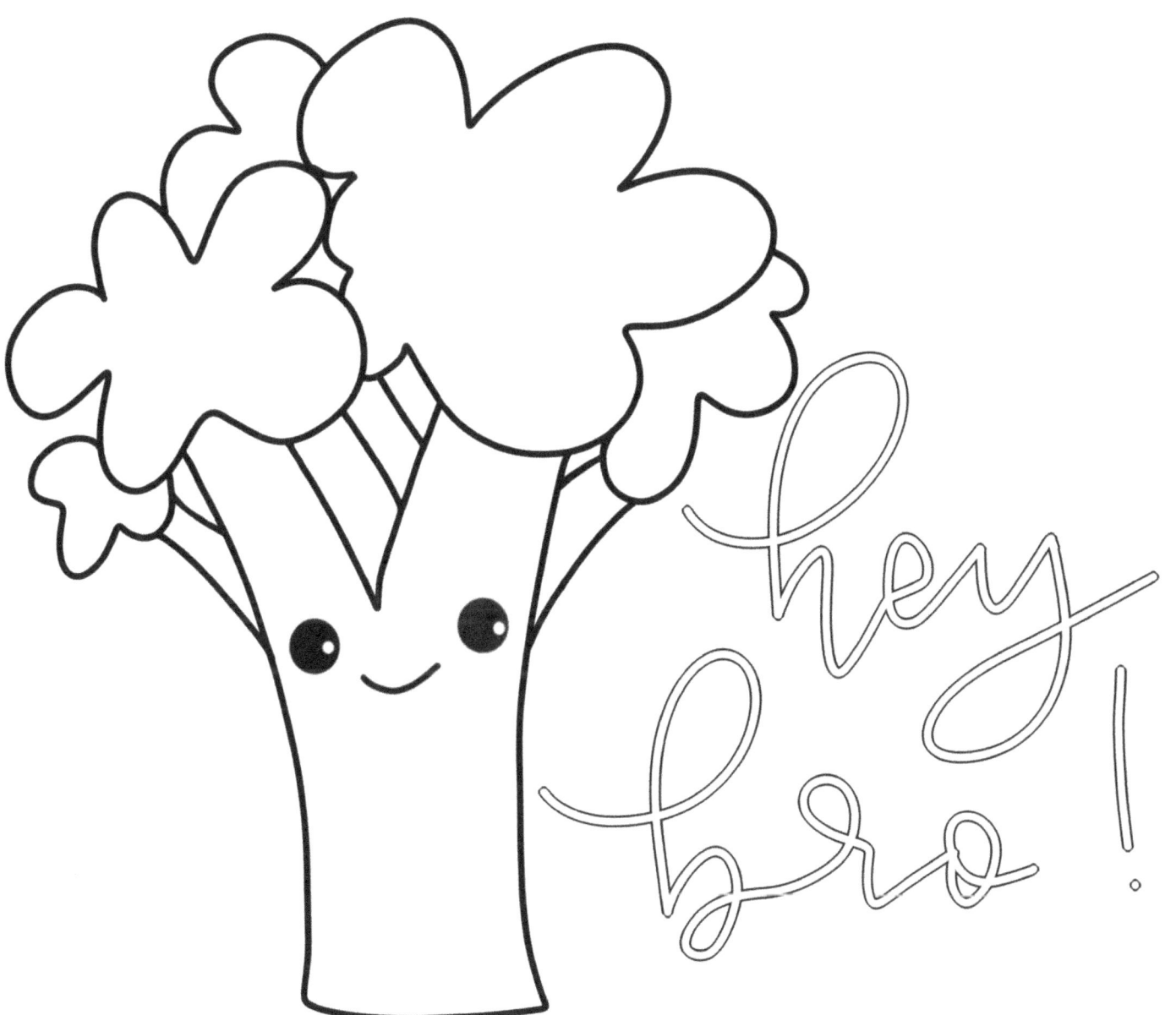

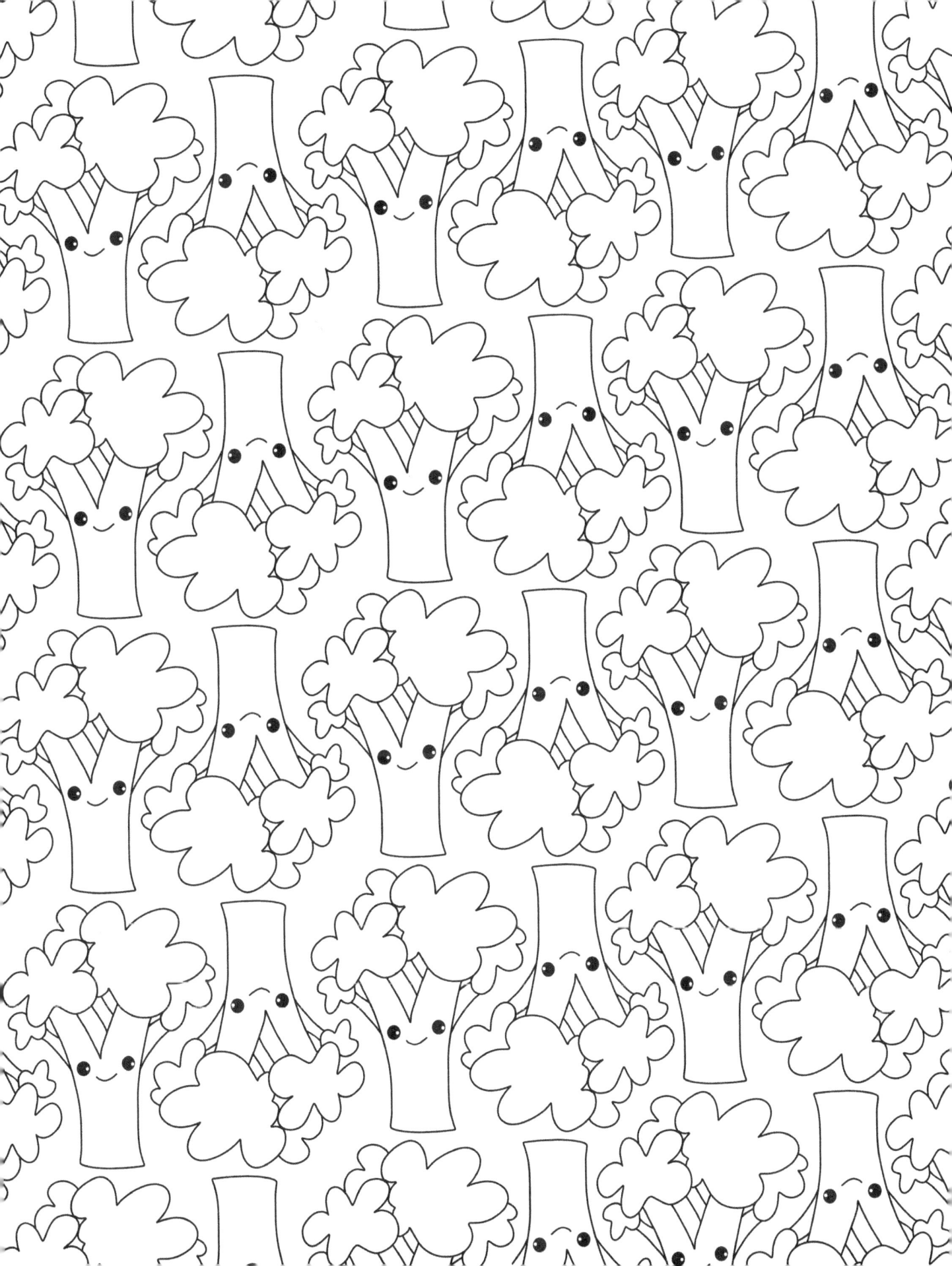

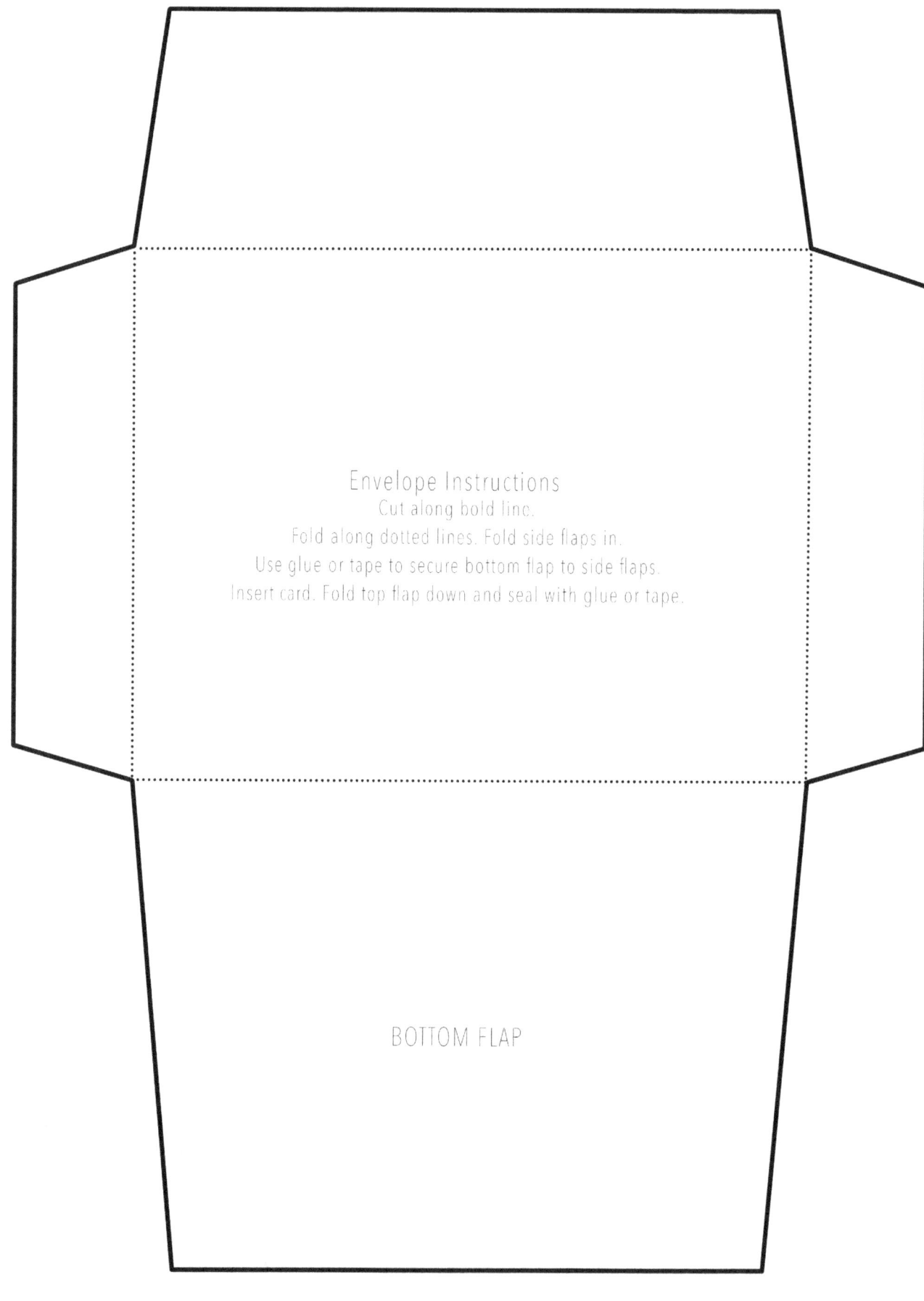

5 LOVE LANGUAGES:

WORDS OF AFFIRMATION:

YOUR TACOS ARE DELICIOUS

QUALITY TIME:

LET'S GO OUT FOR TACOS TOGETHER

ACTS OF SERVICE:

I MADE YOU TACOS

RECEIVING GIFTS:

HERE'S A TACO

PHYSICAL TOUCH:

LET ME HOLD YOU LIKE A TACO

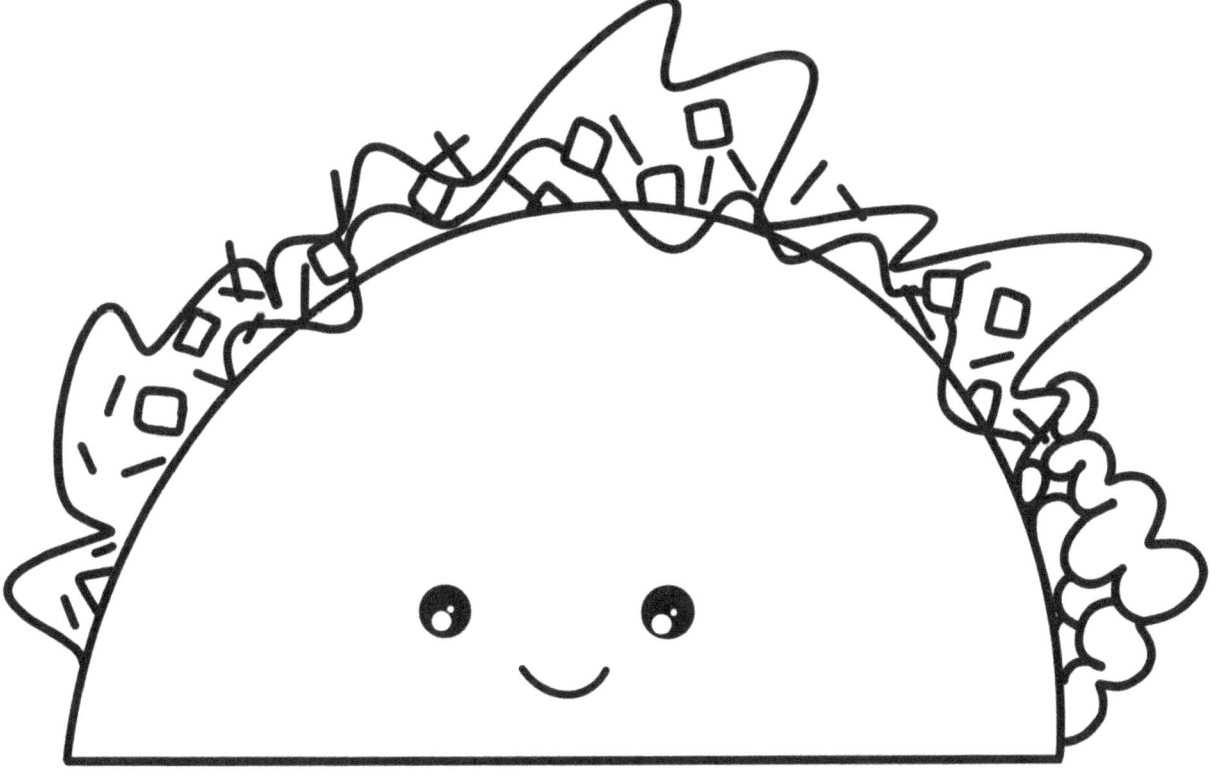

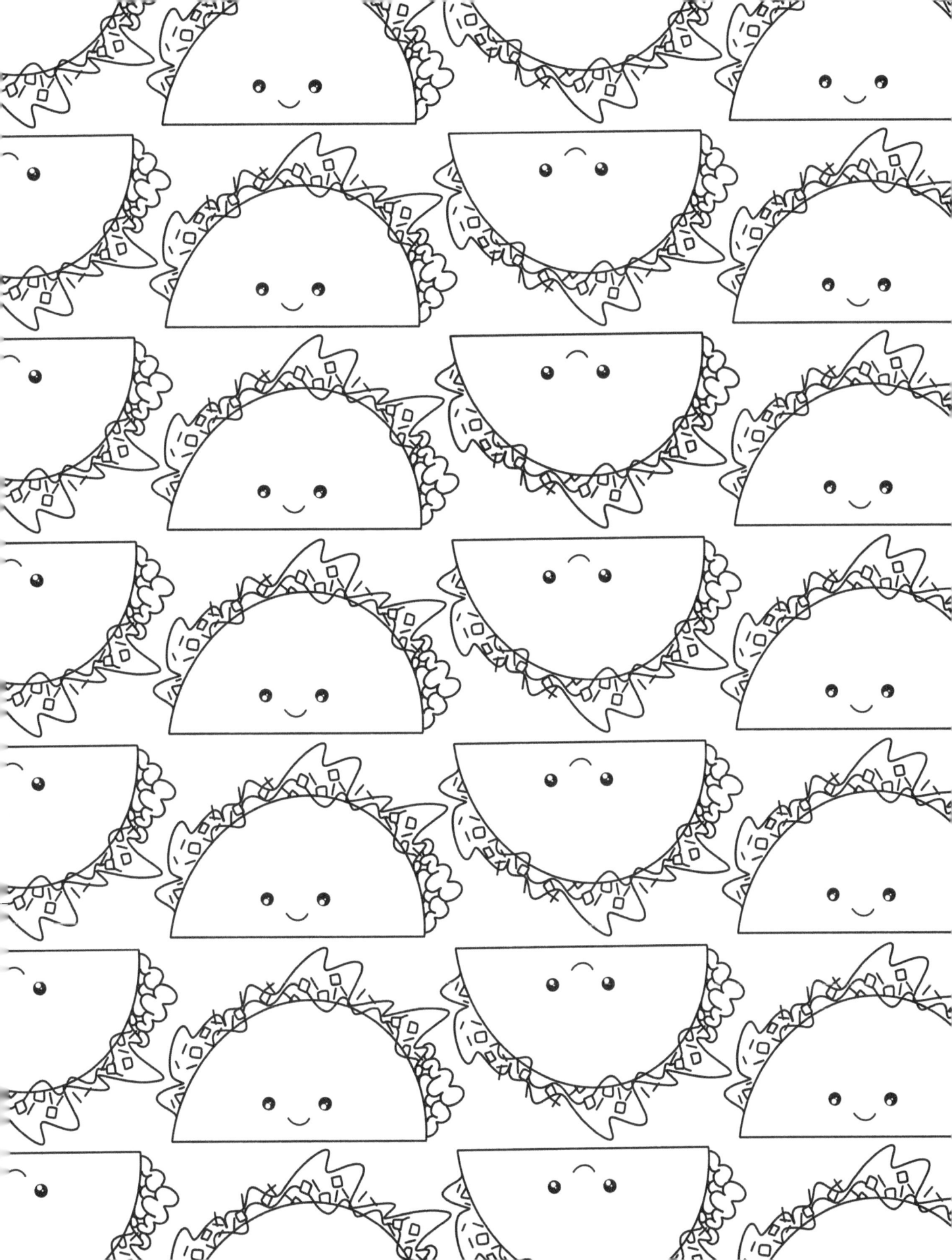

Envelope Instructions

Cut along bold line.
Fold along dotted lines. Fold side flaps in.
Use glue or tape to secure bottom flap to side flaps.
Insert card. Fold top flap down and seal with glue or tape.

BOTTOM FLAP

you are one in a melon

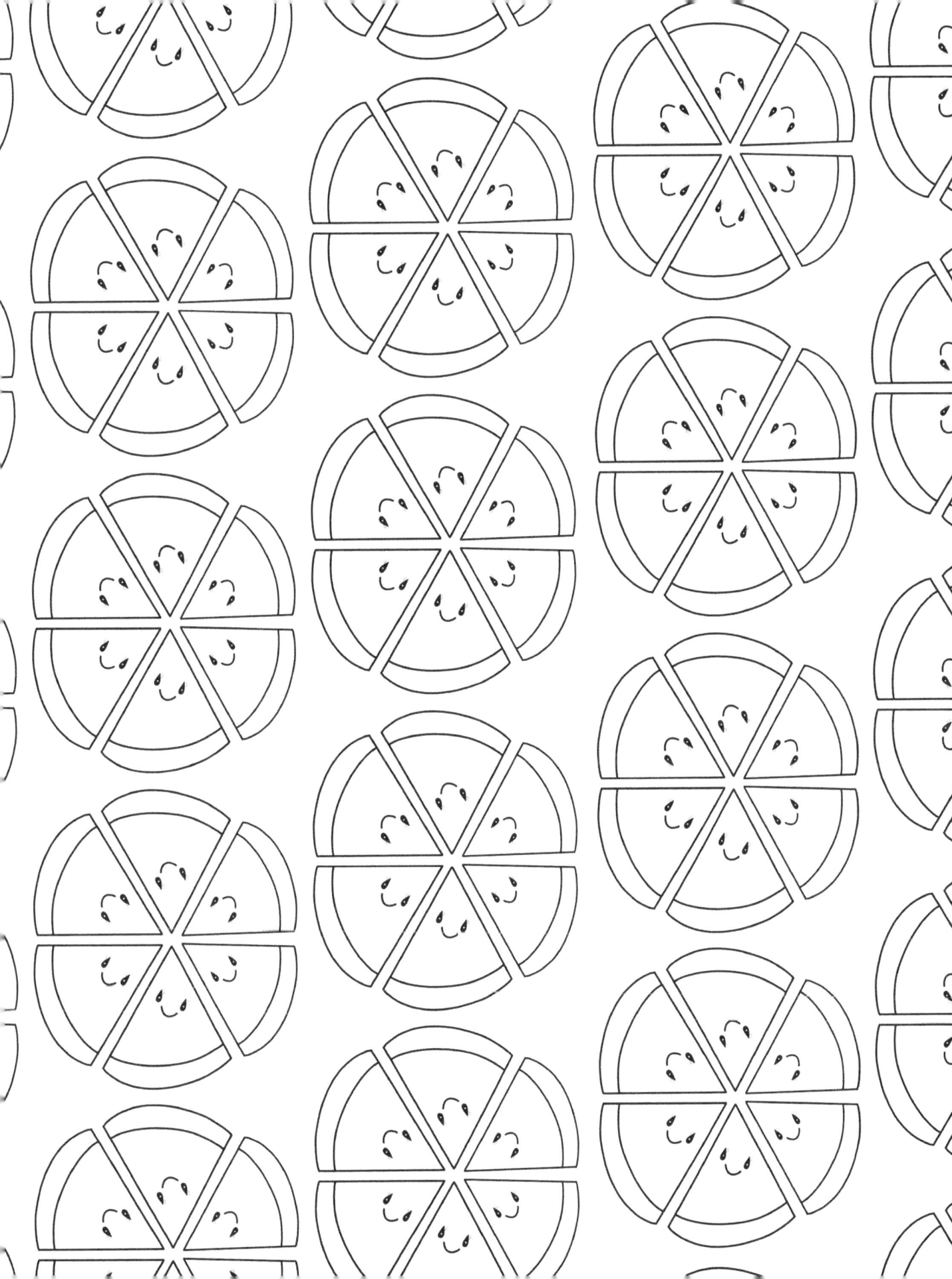

Envelope Instructions
Cut along bold line.
Fold along dotted lines. Fold side flaps in.
Use glue or tape to secure bottom flap to side flaps.
Insert card. Fold top flap down and seal with glue or tape.

BOTTOM FLAP

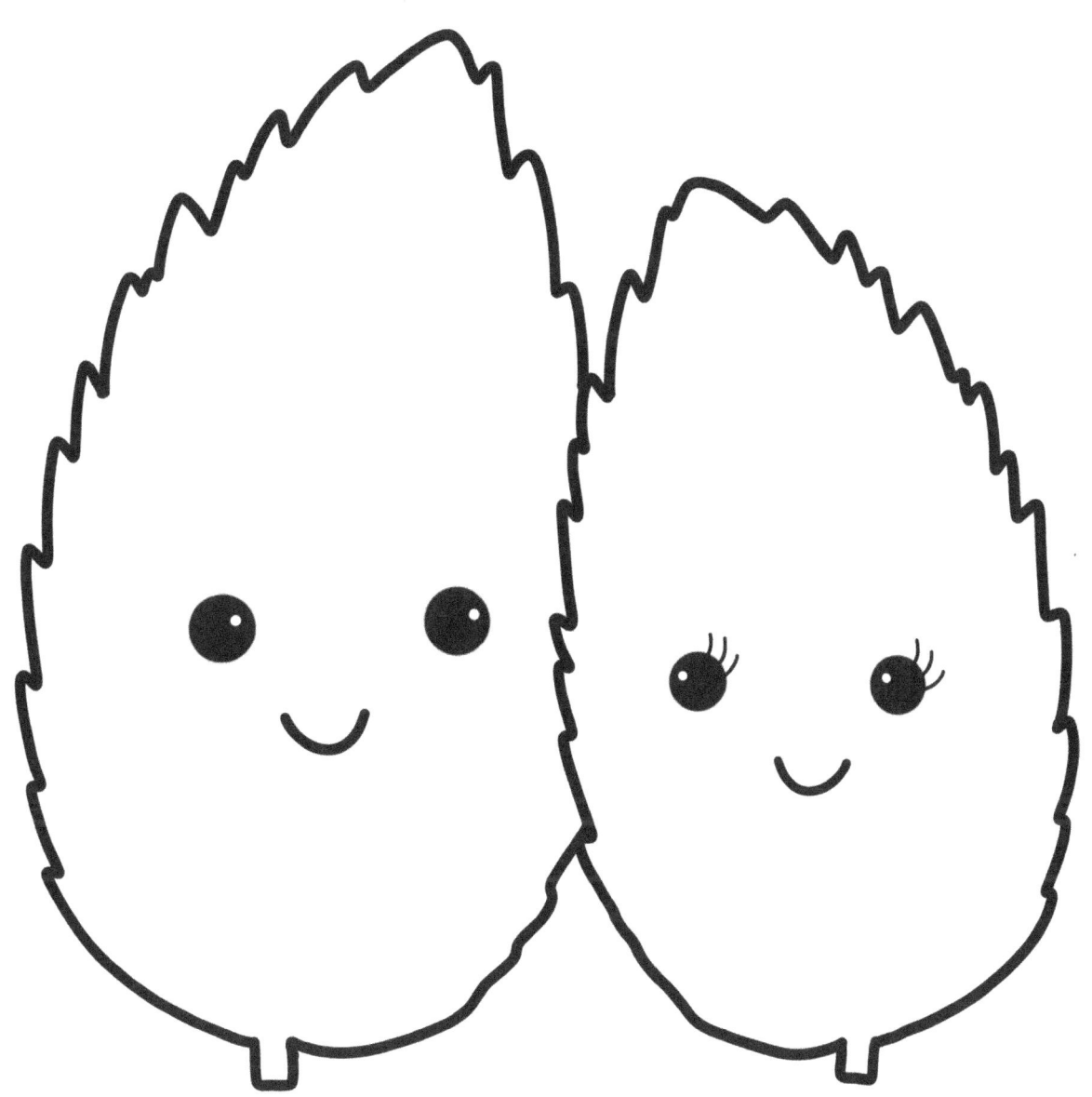

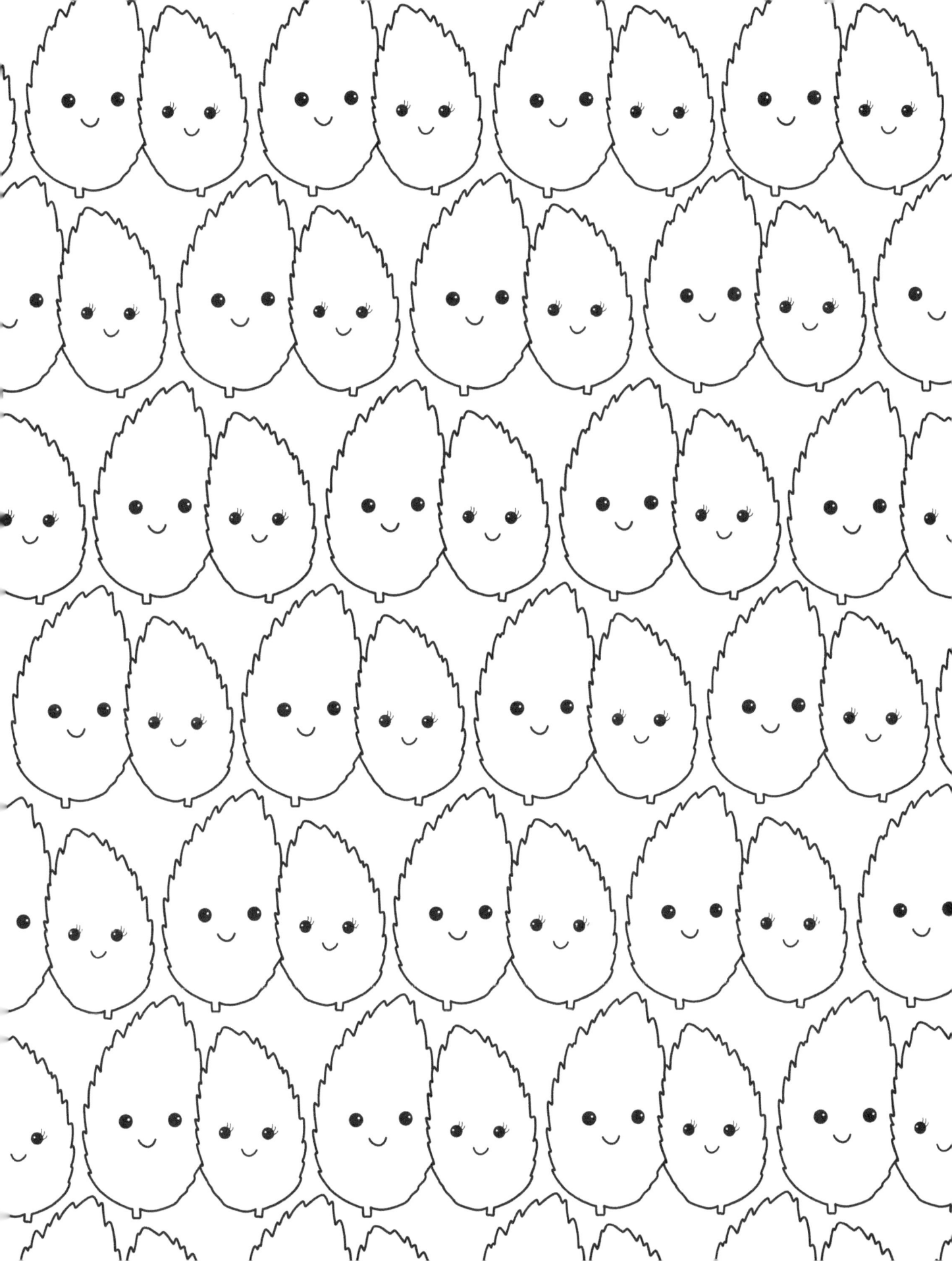

Envelope Instructions

Cut along bold line.

Fold along dotted lines. Fold side flaps in.

Use glue or tape to secure bottom flap to side flaps.

Insert card. Fold top flap down and seal with glue or tape.

BOTTOM FLAP

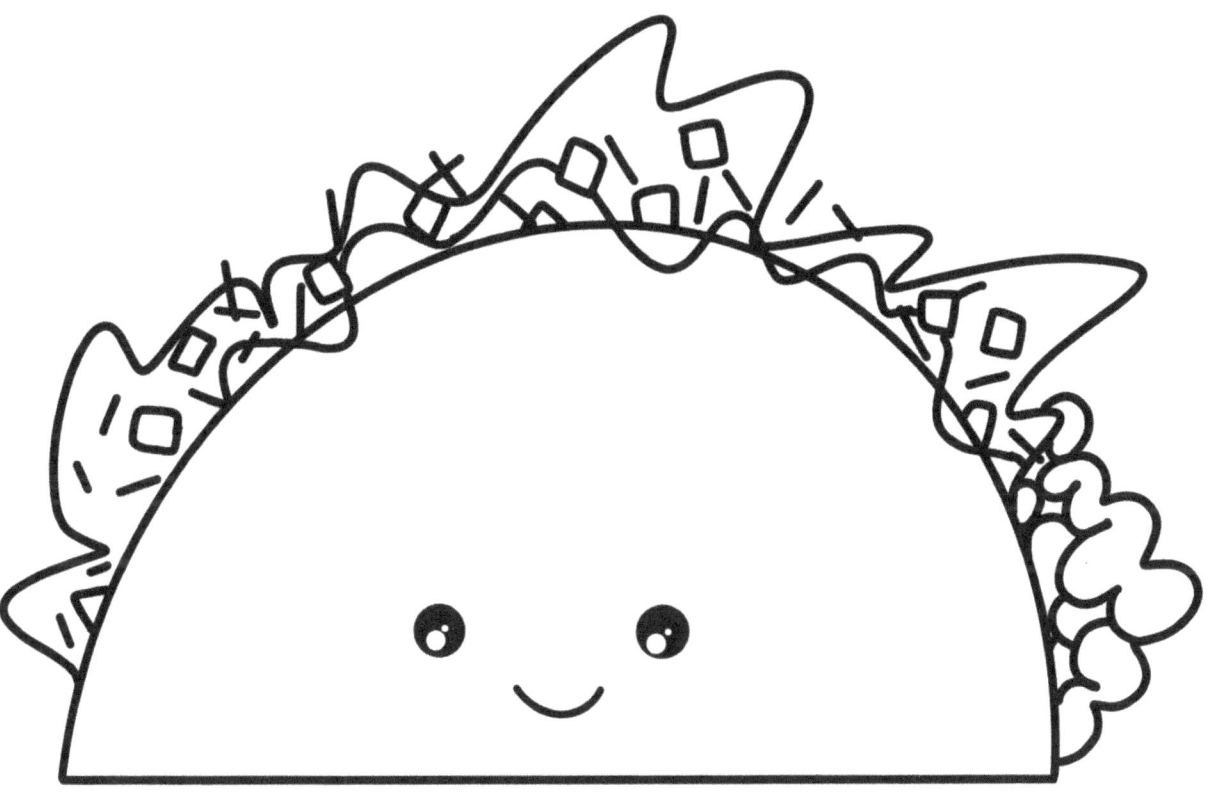

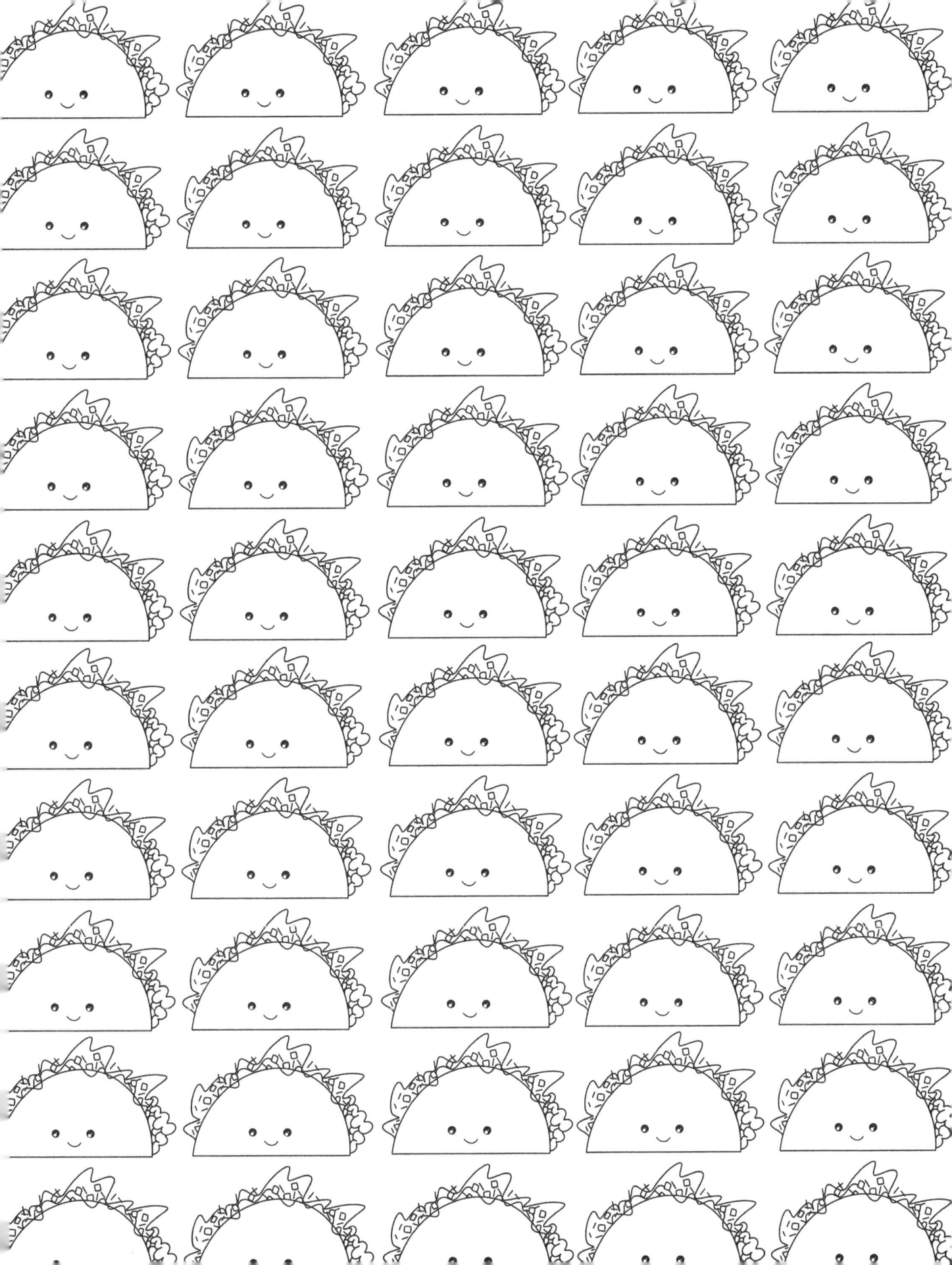

Envelope Instructions
Cut along bold line.
Fold along dotted lines. Fold side flaps in.
Use glue or tape to secure bottom flap to side flaps.
Insert card. Fold top flap down and seal with glue or tape.

BOTTOM FLAP

you can't make everyone happy... you aren't a jar of nutella

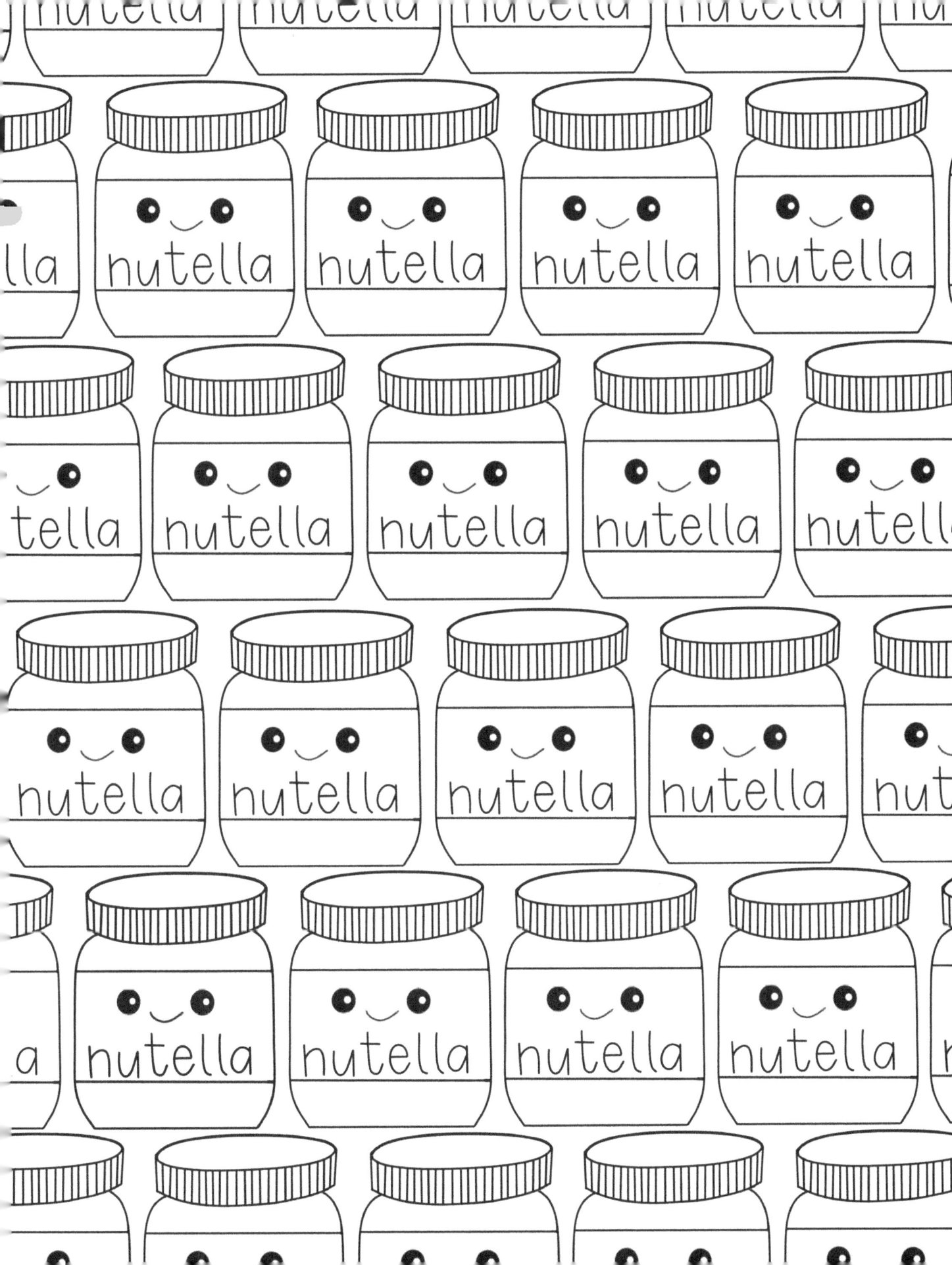

Envelope Instructions
Cut along bold line.
Fold along dotted lines. Fold side flaps in.
Use glue or tape to secure bottom flap to side flaps.
Insert card. Fold top flap down and seal with glue or tape.

BOTTOM FLAP

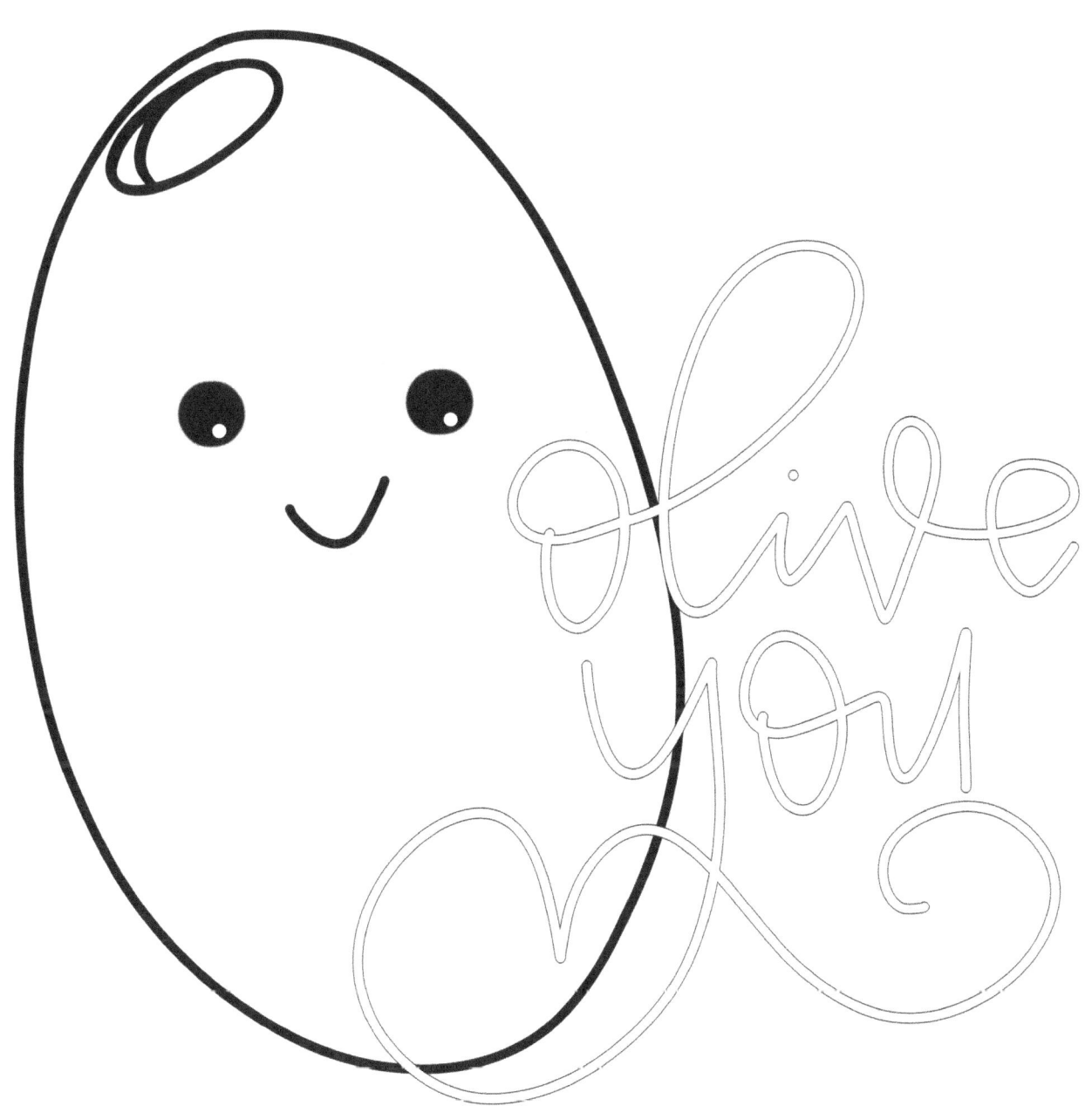

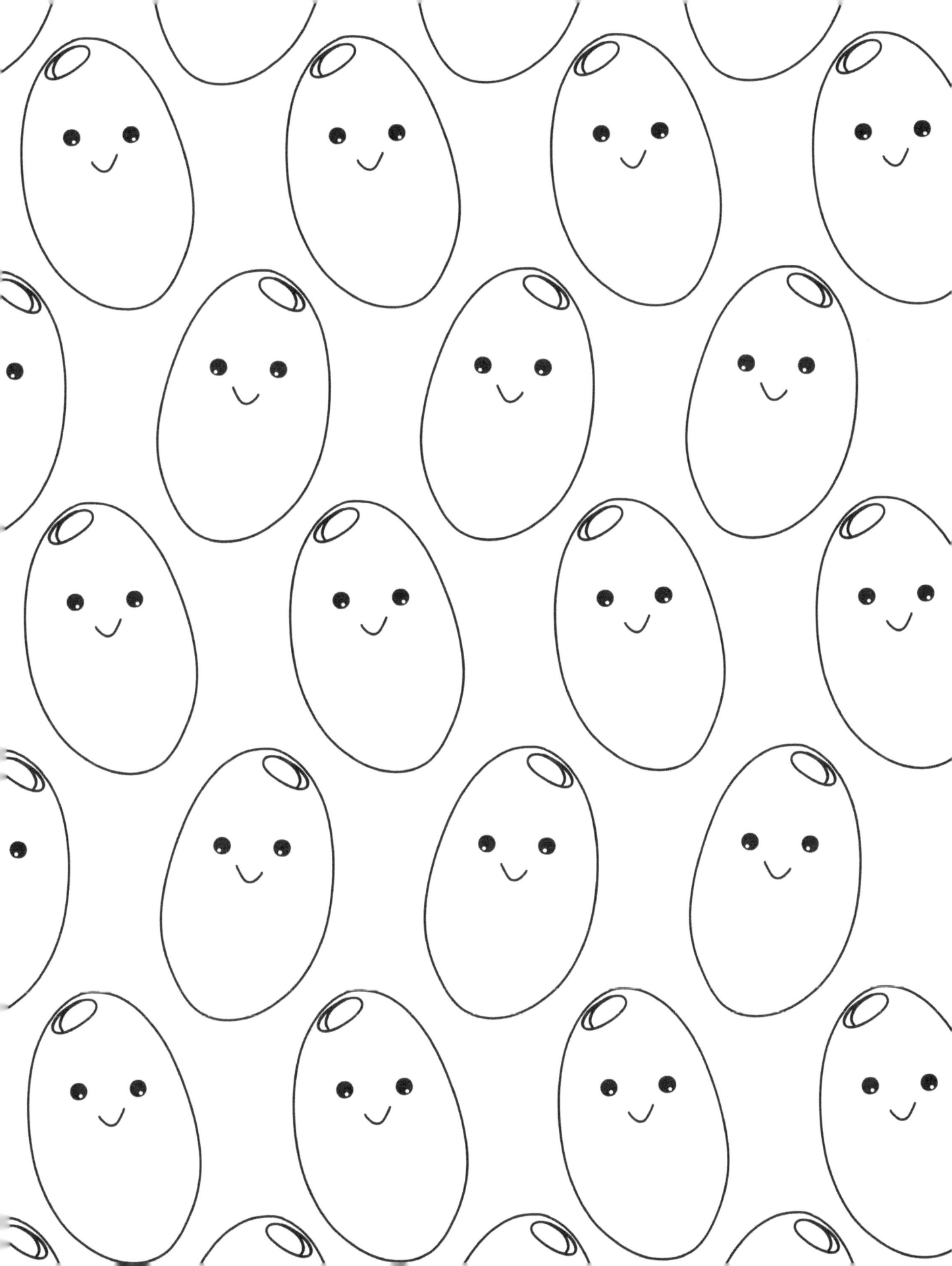

Envelope Instructions

Cut along bold line.
Fold along dotted lines. Fold side flaps in.
Use glue or tape to secure bottom flap to side flaps.
Insert card. Fold top flap down and seal with glue or tape.

BOTTOM FLAP

you're my other half

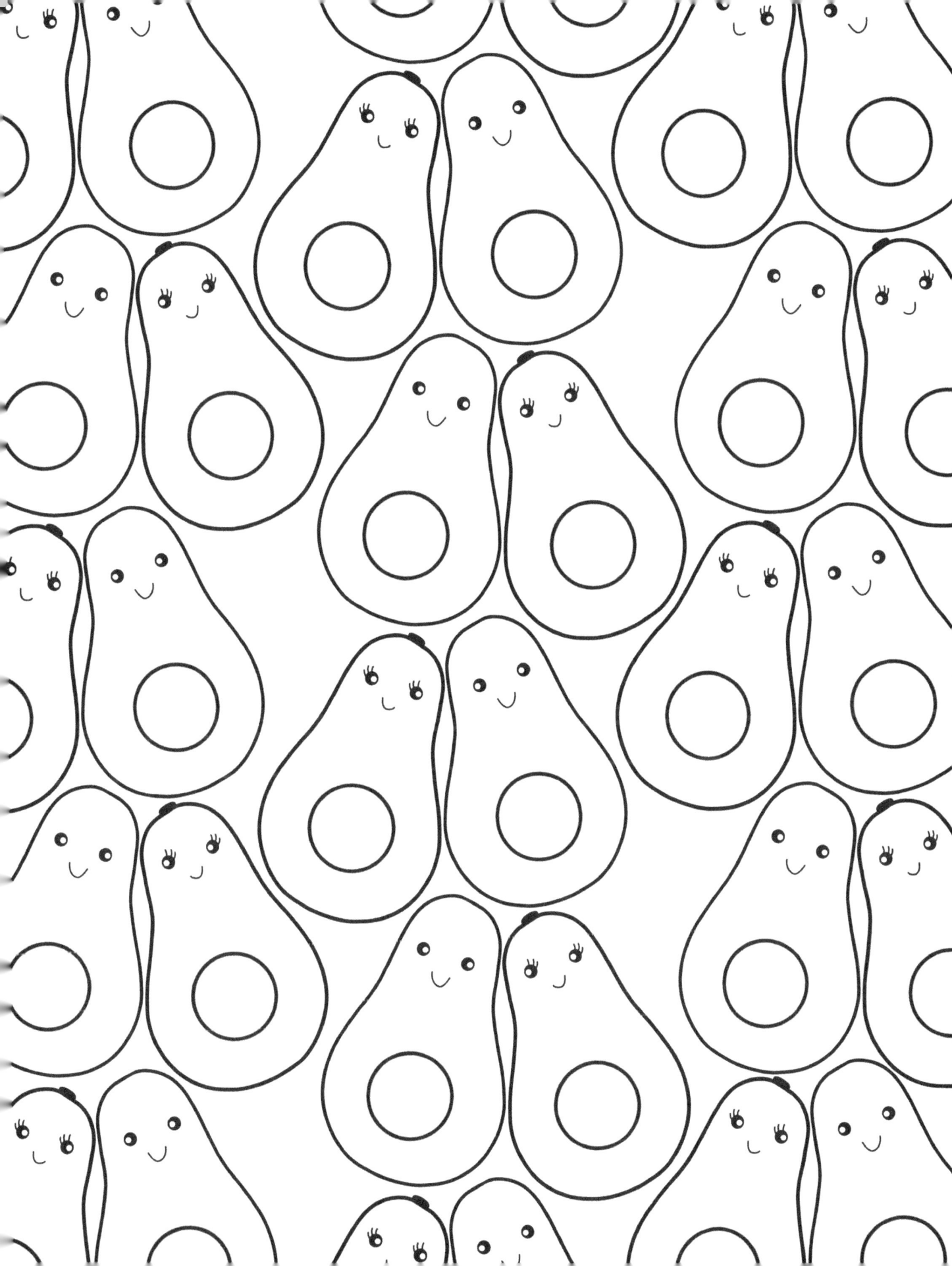

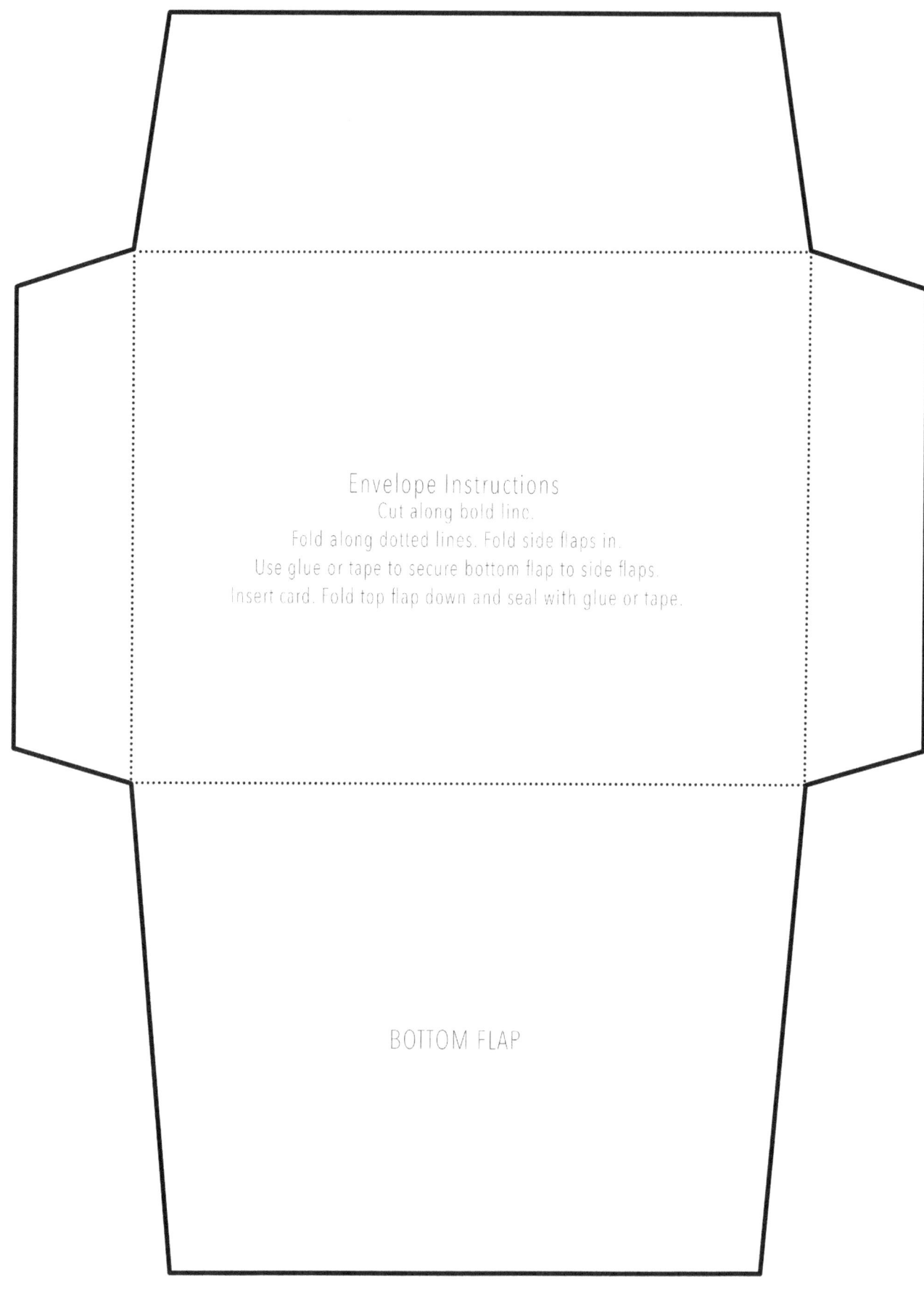

Romaine

calm

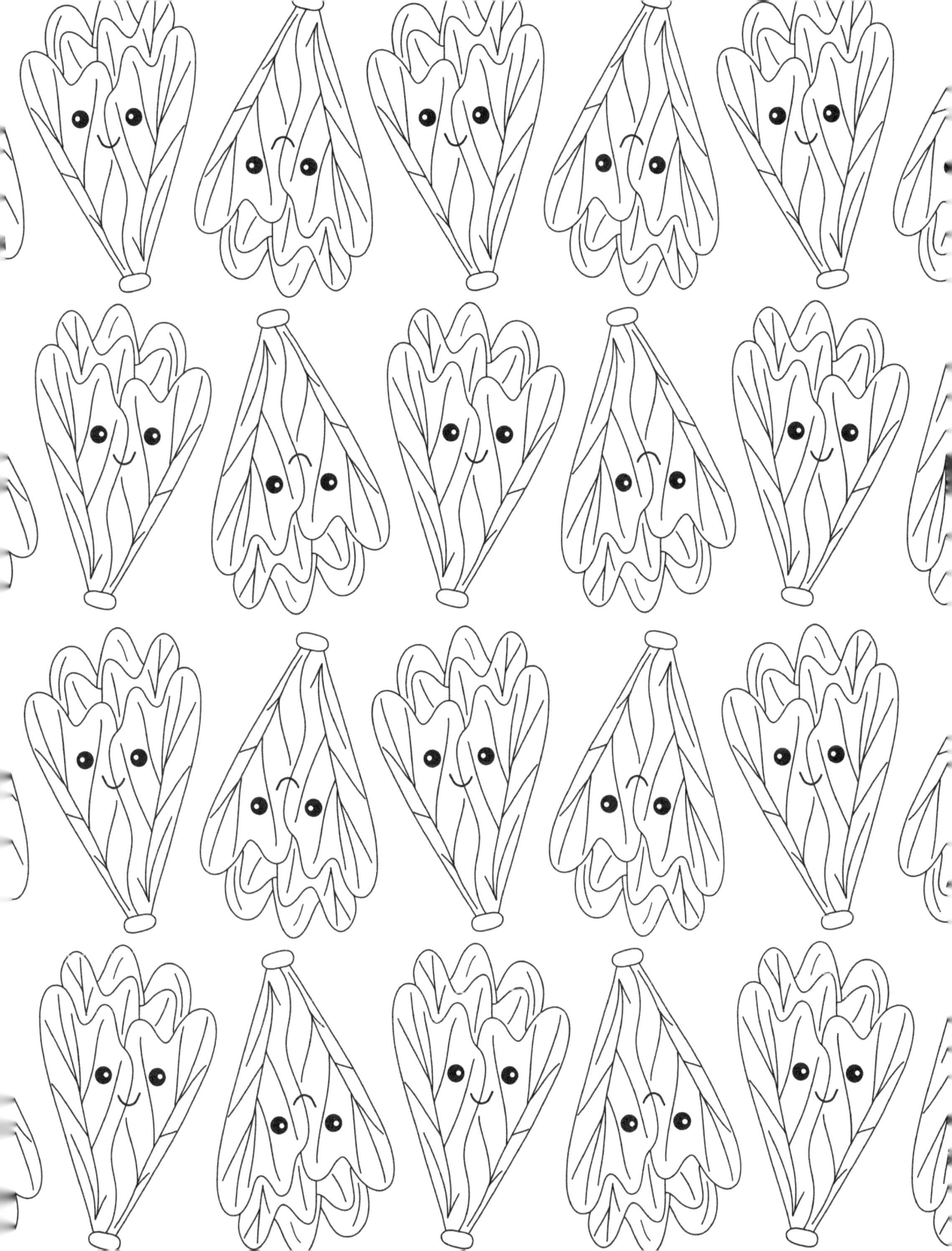

Envelope Instructions

Cut along bold line.
Fold along dotted lines. Fold side flaps in.
Use glue or tape to secure bottom flap to side flaps.
Insert card. Fold top flap down and seal with glue or tape.

BOTTOM FLAP